In Every Generation

Six Pathways to Personal Freedom
Using the Themes of Passover

Six Pathways to Personal Freedom
Using the Themes of Passover

BY KATHERINE ENGLEBARDT, LCSW-R

**In Every Generation: Six Pathways to Personal Freedom
Using the Themes of Passover**

ISBN: 978-0-578-70328-2
First Edition - June 2020

Published by JGU Press. Printed in the USA.

Design & Layout by Carasmatic Design - www.CarasmaticDesign.com

Dedication

Dedicated to my husband, dearest friend, and life partner, Carl, and to our children, family, friends, and teachers. You have been an invaluable part of my life, and I remain grateful for the lessons you continue to teach me and for our being on this journey together.

One good turn
deserves another!
To our dear friends
Marty & Sharon
Be gescendt—
Kathy

Table of Contents

בְּכָל דּוֹר וָדוֹר חַיָּב אָדָם לִרְאוֹת אֶת עַצְמוֹ
כְּאִלּוּ הוּא יָצָא מִמִּצְרַיִם.

"B'chol dor va-dor hayav adam lirot
et atzmo ki-ilu hu yatza mi-mitzrayim.[1] *"*

"In every generation it is mandatory for
each individual to look upon the self as
if personally delivered from Egypt."

1. From the "*Haggadah*," the traditional "telling" of the story of the Jewish People's Exodus from Egypt. This quote is central to Passover and appears in every edition of the Haggadah.

Introduction

What is Personal Freedom? How are we "personally delivered from Egypt" each year?

I believe "Personal Freedom" means that you are free to be your authentic self. You move physically through space and your activities in life to the best of your physical abilities. You are able to think all your thoughts and feel each of your emotions fully, expressing them without fear. Your behaviors are chosen rather than reactive and are not dictated by hurtful personal habits, addictions, or old beliefs. In Personal Freedom, your relationships are healthy and mutually nurturing rather than draining or toxic. Spiritually, you feel a deep connection to a Higher Power or G-d. You know that you are not alone; you know that you are connected to all beings and the universe. It is my hope that reading this book and doing the suggested exercises will clarify and help you walk these Personal Paths to Freedom.

———

Many Jewish holidays offer opportunities for reflection. Two in particular offer a 'new start,' for a new year. We think first of *Rosh Hashanah*, but there is another that follows approximately six months later, *Pesach* or Passover, also referred to as *Chag HaMatzot*, or the Feast of Matzot. For our purposes, Passover, *Pesach*, *Chag HaMatzot*, and the Feast of Unleavened Bread or *Matzot* are used interchangeably.

Many people have never thought of *Pesach* as the start of a new year, but it occurs on the 15th day of the first month of the Jewish calendar, *Nisan* (in the spring), with *Rosh Hashanah* taking place in the seventh month, *Tishrei* (in the fall).

Why the need for a second new year? Perhaps G-d knew that, even with the best of intentions, we would maintain many of our shortcomings and need to reassess our thoughts and behaviors and start again. And we would need this opportunity sooner vs. later.

During Elul, the month before *Rosh Hashanah*, we prepare for the coming High Holidays. Wanting a meaningful experience, you do not just walk into the synagogue on the first day of *Rosh Hashanah* and begin to think about who you are and what your behaviors have been during the past year. Hopefully, we look back at our year, review, assess, and plan for repentance and a fresh start. Starting with the month of Elul, the *shofar* is blown. Wake up!! It's time!! As we enter the High Holidays, we attend *shul*, pray, and ask for forgiveness from our friends, from G-d, and we start anew. If you have not prepared previously, you are given the Ten Days of Awe (the intermediary days between *Rosh Hashanah* and *Yom Kippur*), before then making atonement on *Yom Kippur*. But the High Holidays are even more meaningful if you have been preparing for them during the month of Elul, if not all year.

Following the High Holidays, our days take on their own demands and struggles. The immediacy of repentance and renewal fades with shortening days. We move into late fall, and then the bright lights of *Chanukah* during the darkest days of winter. We backslide, we regress, we sin again, and then again.

Signs of spring emerge, and with Purim we rejoice and party, grateful that we, as a people, have been saved once more. We wear our masks, masks that the days of *Pesach* will ask us to shed.

We prepare for the days of *Chag Hamatzot.* We clean our homes, get out our special Passover dishes and utensils, make festive meals, read the *Haggadah* at our Seders, and ask ourselves:

Who am I, really? To whom and to what am I still enslaved? Who is the Master of my time and space? How will my spirit leave *mitzrayim,* the narrow, confining spaces, and emerge a free person this year?

Will I ???

The *Haggadah* tells us that we must each relive the Exodus as if we were there, as if we personally experienced slavery and emerged from Egypt free people. And truly, each year we ARE there. Each year we hold onto beliefs, habits, and ways of thinking and behaving that keep us enslaved. We must ready ourselves to leave these old ways. We are always growing and learning. Like Jacob, we are again wrestling with these questions of identity to emerge a different person, creating our own exodus from our beleaguered ways.

If we are to truly experience and enjoy *Pesach*, each year we must take advantage of our opportunity to leave slavery again, to leave *mitzrayim* (our personal Egypts or "narrow places") and courageously step into the sea, and be free.

The words and exercises in this book are a guide to help you experience the true liberation of Passover. Just as the Jewish people were told to prepare, that the day of the Exodus was coming, you know that the day of Passover is coming, too. You must prepare ahead, move through the experience, and review what it has meant afterwards. It will be your chance to celebrate your freedom once again. However, just as it took forty years of wandering in the desert to cleanse the slave mentality, you cannot accomplish this during one or two seders or even years. It is a lifelong process of re-experiencing and re-commitment each year.

Similarly, if *Pesach* is to truly have personal meaning, you have much preparation to do. You rid your home, car, and place of work of physical *hametz* (leavening and products that contain leaven or rising agents). You bring out special dishes, utensils, and serving pieces that are used only at this time of year. You cook special foods, loving the taste during the first days, and yearning to be done by the end! During the seders you recline, read the *Haggadah*, drink wine or grape juice, and glean new meanings of the *Haggadah* through discussions with friends and family. These are truly different nights and meals, but why – to what end? And is it really over 8 days later?

The weeks of preparing for Passover gives us time to go inward and reflect on the *hametz* in our lives. Discovering what personal freedom means will vary for each individual. It is my hope that the exercises in this book will help you prepare your inner world for the holiday of Passover. As a continuation of your work during the month of Elul and the High Holidays, this book is a guide integrating the themes of Passover with what I term the "Six Pathways to Personal Freedom."

What you will find in this book:

Chapter 1 defines the term *"hametz"* as it is usually understood – the biblical sources from which the term comes and the command to rid our homes of *hametz* before the first seder, the beginning of Passover. We are commanded to rid our homes of any leavening (*hametz*) before the ioliday of Passover begins and to eat matzah and *"kosher l'Pesach"* foods hroughout the holiday.[2]

Chapter 2 takes the term *"hametz"* and expands it (pun intended) to dentify that which weighs on you, is excess, and/or keeps you enslaved. The Six Pathways to Personal Freedom are introduced.

In **Chapter 3** you will learn activities and exercises to enter these pathways and let go of what no longer serves you.

Chapter 4 brings you to personal choice regarding what you have earned. What will you keep and bring out of Egypt? What will you release and leave behind?

It is my hope that this book will guide you to experience a joyous and meaningful Passover that will have lasting significance through the following months and year. It will aid in your personal growth from *Pesach* to *Rosh Hashanah* and then once again to *Pesach*, thereby helping to bring you into more meaningful celebrations and insights into our continual opportunities for new beginnings, rebirth, and cycles of freedom.

---

2. BIblical sources of *Hametz*: Exodus 12:7, 12:34, 13:3-16, Leviticus 23: 6-8.

Chapter 1

What is Hametz?

The statement in the *Haggadah* that every generation must experience Passover each year as if *we* are slaves who will emerge as free people is central to *Pesach* and is the core of this book. We read this statement at every seder, as we fulfill the commandment to retell the Passover story in every generation. As we listen to our youngest family member recite the Four Questions, perhaps we add these additional questions to our *Haggadah*:

"What does this mean to me? How can I have personally left Egypt? And what does that have to do with my life today?"

To answer these questions, let us begin with the commandment to rid our homes of *hametz*. The term *"hametz"* means "leavening," and, as referred to in the Bible[3], is a known and measurable item. It refers to any ingredient that causes the fermentation or rising of food. Leavening also increases acidity and sourness.

3. David L. Lieber, Sr. Ed., *Etz Chayim, Torah and Commentary* (New York: The Jewish Publication Society, 1985), 382.

At the time of the original Exodus, we did not have time to allow our bread to rise. We left Egypt in haste, with unrisen or flat bread. To commemorate this event, we are commanded to rid our homes of any leavening (*hametz*) before the holiday of Passover begins and to eat *matzah* and only "*kosher l'Pesach*" foods and drinks throughout the holiday.

We can further define "our homes" to include our physical and spiritual homes. *Hametz* is in our foods, and is also within us. Some scholars suggest *hametz* "also symbolizes a puffiness of self, an inflated personality, an egocentricity that threatens to eclipse the essential personality of the individual."[4]

Let us look at the ways in which *hametz* was defined by biblical scholars.

In rabbinic literature, leaven is often used as a metaphor for the evil inclination or *yetzer ha-ra*.[5]

Rabbi Kerry Olitzky cites Rabbi Arthur Waskow who called this kind of *hametz*, the "swollen sourness in our lives" that "lurks menacingly in the recesses of the soul."[6]

> ...*Hametz is also the baggage we carry from broken promises, failed relationships, and personal disappointments that weigh heavily on us. It is the refuse of daily living, the residual stuff that emerges from poor decisions, mistakes in judgment, and mortal failure.*[7]

Rabbi Olitzky suggests that the preparation of our hearts and spirits for Passover takes as much effort as we assert in physically cleaning our homes.

> *Just as one removes the leaven by the light of the candle, one should eliminate the evil that dwells within, searching the heart by the light of the soul, which is the 'candle of G-d.' Only with Divine light are we even*

---

4. Rabbi Kerry M. Olitzky, *Preparing Your Heart for Passover* (Philadelphia: The Jewish Publication Society, 2002), 3-4.
5. Olitzky, *Preparing Your Heart for Passover*, 3.
6. Olitzky, *Preparing Your Heart for Passover*, 3.
7. Olitzky, *Preparing Your Heart for Passover*, 5.

able to see the hametz that is buried in our soul. And only through that same light are we able to incinerate it.[8]

Preparing for Passover is about removing the physical and spiritual leaven from our homes and lives. The cleaning of our homes should also be a cleansing of our spirits, giving new meaning to our personal experience of leaving Egypt and slavery.

My interpretation of *hametz* extends to **anything that no longer serves us, but instead keeps us enslaved.** Anything that is excessive, "puffed up," sour, acidic, or otherwise detrimental to our well-being and growth as free people, may be considered *hametz*. It is something to remove from ourselves as we go from slavery to freedom.

For example, when I recognize that I am carrying too much responsibility for others, that is *hametz* that I need to let go of. When I am carrying anger, past hurts, and resentments towards others, that needs to be released, so that I may be free of old negativity. When I am acting out of a sense of guilt vs. a willing desire to do something, that is behavioral *hametz*. When I feel haughty or arrogant, that is ego *hametz*. When I see that physically my home is cluttered and I can't think straight, the clutter is *hametz*. Freedom comes when I clear my spaces and release what I no longer use or need.

Reading and completing the exercises in this book, *"In Every Generation," Six Pathways to Personal Freedom*, will help you to identify what is meant by your personal *"hametz."* By approaching *hametz* through the pathways of your physical, mental, emotional, behavioral, relational, and spiritual lives, you will be guided to identify and release that which no longer serves you, but keeps you enslaved. You will find Personal Freedom.

In the following chapter, we will look at how *hametz* shows up in ourselves and introduce the model of the Whole Person Wheel, which will guide us on the Six Pathways to Personal Freedom.

---

8. Olitzky, *Preparing Your Heart for Passover*, 3-4.

Chapter 2

Identifying Hametz in Ourselves by Using the Six Pathways to Personal Freedom

Ridding ourselves of *hametz*, means we must leave *"mitzrayim,"* or "Egypt," in ancient times, now the narrow places in our hearts, minds, behaviors and souls.

To quote Rabbi Irving Greenberg:

> *Freedom is not given in a day or reached overnight. The house of bondage is within you unless you are psychologically ready to be free… people must prepare themselves mentally and physically before they can relive the liberation experience.*[9]

But how are we to do this?

9. Rabbi Irving Greenberg, *The Jewish Way, Living the Holidays* (New York: TouchstoneBooks, 1988), 41.

It is my experience that starting with the more concrete, physical, sensation-able (in the manner of experiencing through our senses) is an easier task than beginning with the ephemeral, i.e., spirit or soul. So let us begin there.

The model I propose is one I learned many years ago at a conference for Adult Children of Alcoholics. The presenter, Sharon Wegsheider-Cruse, used what she called the "Whole Person Wheel."[10] This is a model that I have adapted to illustrate how the Physical, Mental, Emotional, Behavioral, Relational, and Spiritual parts of ourselves are integrated into one full human being. I call these the "Six Pathways to Personal Freedom" and refer to this model throughout this book. Using this model and the worksheets provided, we can enter the integrated circle that defines ourselves via any one pathway to further recognize who we are and the choices we make in life.

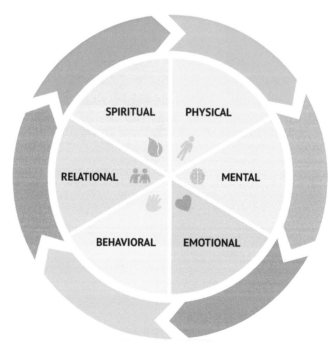

10. Sharon Wegscheider-Cruse, *Another Chance, Hope and Health for the Alcoholic Family* (Palo Alto: Science and Behavior Books, Inc., 1981), 11.

This concept suggests that we are not just our conscious minds or our physical bodies, but that we are integrated beings that fuse all the parts of ourselves into an inter-dependent whole. This became a seminal model in my work with individuals, in workshops, and with groups. The pathways are all connected, and we can begin at any one point. For our purposes, we will use the Six Pathways identified, in the order listed above: Physical, Mental, Emotional, Behavioral, Relational, and Spiritual.

Pathway #1: Physical

Here we look at our physical beings. Some parts of our physical beings manifest in our general health, the food we eat, the way we move, our breathing, our health, our sexuality, the effects of stress on our bodies, our sleep, our general self-care or lack thereof, and our physical environment.

Using Worksheet #1 on page 55: Take a moment to think about what it is that keeps you enslaved physically. Is it the food you eat, the amounts, the type of food? Do you feel heavy or over-burdened physically? Perhaps you don't want to eat sugar, but find you have a difficult time passing it up when offered.

Or are there addictive substances or activities in your life that you want to release?

Do you use your cell phone, social media, and technology to engage with others, or are you on automatic, being compelled to have your cell phone at all times?

Can you let go of food that is detrimental to your health (i.e. sugar, processed food, excess). Have you been wanting to eat according to the laws of *kashrut*? Can you make the commitment to eat more healthfully and/or to keep kosher this year? What does that look like? What small steps can you take to bring you closer to your ideal?

While this is not an "addictions recovery program," It *can* be helpful in recognizing what is keeping you enslaved. Certainly rushing around Egypt to find sugar, chocolate, alcohol, cigarettes, or your cell phone, and then having to carry those will not make your journey easier. We need to release the burdens we carry and lighten our load for the journey ahead.

Some other questions to ask yourself regarding your physical experience may be:

- How is your environment? Is it crowded, cluttered, in disarray? Do you need to let go of some of the physical objects in your home and life?

- Do you need to rearrange or organize your environment so that it works for vs. hinders you? How can you make your home and/or work environment more helpful to you?

- What is your relationship to your cell phone? Is it a tool that frees you or an object to which you are enslaved?

- How do you move physically? What brings you comfortable freedom of movement?

- Do you practice relaxation and deep breathing? Are you attuned to the stress in your muscles and able to release that?

The eight days of the Feast of Unleavened Bread are a good time to introduce healthy eating, movement, and breathing. Our homes are cleared and cleaned. Our environment is clearer, simplified. Why not put only kosher and healthy foods back on our shelves? You have cleared out pots, pans, dishes and foods. This is a good time to *kasher* (purify by means of dietary laws) these items and utensils before putting them back on the shelves.

Perhaps you want to add more relaxation and movement into your life. There are many ways of incorporating breathing, relaxation, stretching, and physical activity into your life. A daily practice of finding a quiet space, allowing no interruptions, and simply sitting in a relaxed manner watching your breath enter and leave your body can bring peace and a freer state of mind and body.

Pathway #2: Mental

Some of our mental processes include memory, the formulation of new ideas, thought patterns, and imagination. What are our thought patterns? Everyone talks to themselves. We need to tune into what it is we are saying to ourselves. Our thoughts influence all aspects of our health and freedom. Pay attention to what you are telling yourself. Are you kind and nurturing, as you would be to a young child? Or, like many of us, are you negative, harsh, and critical? Are you unforgiving of your own past behaviors?

Using Worksheet #2 on page 57: Take a moment to write down some of your disturbing thoughts. Do you catch yourself saying negative statements to yourself? Perhaps your mind tells you, "You can't do that!" or "Who do you think you are?"

Or you may be dwelling on past hurts and insults, unable to let them go. This is a mental form of enslavement that we are continuing, perhaps automatically. If you pay attention to your thoughts, you may find you are a harsh taskmaster. **But those masters were in Egypt. It is time to leave them there:**

> *When we can wash ourselves clean of the debris that clutters our minds and our memories, then we can relive the experience of our people; we can return to the desert and begin the journey home again.*[11]

---

11. Olitzky, *Preparing Your Heart for Passover*, 18.

Pathway #3: Emotional

There are many charts or lists to help you identify human emotions. "Happy," "peaceful," "irritable," "angry," "sad," "joyful," "inferior," "envious," and "loving" are just a few of our hourly and daily emotions. There is a reason these feelings are called "E-motions." Our feelings are meant to be experienced and acted upon, not just felt or pushed away once we feel them.

Personal Freedom Tip

Carry around a small notepad and jot down what you are feeling at any given time during a certain day. Learn to recognize and name your feelings.

If you pay attention, you will most likely notice that your emotions fluctuate regularly. They seem to arise from outside ourselves in response to an action from someone else, but in reality *our emotions are a result of our own thinking.* Using a Cognitive-Behavioral psychotherapy model:[12] **"A" happens, "B" I have a thought, and then "C" a feeling arises from that thought.**

Many people think that "A" happens and I feel "C". But as you pay close attention to your self-talk, you will find that "A" (an event, perhaps even a memory or another thought) happens, "B" *I have a thought*, and then "C" a feeling arises.

What is important is that you *allow* these emotions to surface, *recognize* them, and *choose* how you wish to respond. If you simply react, you are a slave to that emotion. But you do not have to remain a slave. You can build in a pause, a chance to feel the emotion and then decide how to respond. You are the master, not the slave, by simply sitting with that feeling, listening to your thoughts, choosing a response, or choosing not to respond. Instead of a "knee-jerk" reaction, you choose to release that

---

12. For greater understanding of Cognitive-Behavioral theory and psychotherapy, see works by pioneers of Cognitive-Behavioral Psychotherapy, Albert Ellis and Aaron Beck.

emotion in a beneficial way, some of which will be discussed when we look at exercises on breathing and clearing our minds.

Emotional freedom happens when you feel your emotions and choose your responses. You are no longer a slave to your emotions, reacting and then regretting that behavior. You are able to validate what you feel and then choose how you wish to respond.

Pathway #4: Behavioral

Again, when you are reacting vs. choosing your behaviors, you are enslaved. Perhaps during *Yom Kippur*, you identified a behavior for which you said an "*Al Cheyt*."[13] Then what? Have you used your learning during the High Holidays to actually repent and make amends? Have you made the appropriate apology to another and changed your behavior? Have you said, "This I will no longer do," and then put safeguards up to ensure that you don't?[14]

Some examples of behaviors that no longer serve you can be gossip, cruelty to others, unfair business practices, lying, always trying to be right, arguing, and/or refusing to see another's point of view.

As with our emotions, it is important to own and accept our behaviors. There can be no change without this first step. We need to have a loving attitude towards ourselves as we examine how we have behaved. That is in the past. That is a behavior that no longer serves us. It is time to let it go and be free.

As with the other pathways, we cannot expect perfection or instantaneous healing. It is a start to acknowledge the behavior and begin a plan that will allow you to release it.

---

13. From the High Holiday liturgy. Prayer asking for forgiveness from G-d for past thoughts and behaviors.
14. See Maimonides levels of apology and forgiveness for an excellent model on owning behaviors and making amends.

Pathway #5: Relational

Who are your Pharaohs today?

How do you interact with others? Are you truly a free person, or are you subject to control by another? Do you surround yourself with people who are loving and kind? Are there relationships that you need to remove from your life because they no longer serve your well-being? Again, the first step you need to take is to **acknowledge what *is* vs. being in denial.**

Not all troublesome relationships need to be totally released in order to heal and be free. There may be family and friend relationships that are challenging that you want to keep. However, you also want them to have less impact on your well-being. You can make choices here, too. You can lessen the time you spend with someone. You can see a person on your own terms, when you are feeling strong and able to ward off any toxicity they might invite you to experience. Or you may decide this is not someone you want to have in your life right now. Perhaps you will rebuild that relationship at a later time, when you are more comfortable in your freedom and more skilled at looking out for yourself. For now, being free means you no longer tolerate any unkind behaviors, verbal, physical, or emotional abuse from others. You have feet. You are free. You can walk away.

Pathway #6: Spiritual

Do you feel connected to something greater than yourself? Are you living only in a "this worldly" experience? Do you allow yourself to meditate, to pray, to get out of your ego and experience that you are intertwined with all humanity? What blocks you from experiencing a Higher Source or G-d? Have you shut that off, staying in your own mind vs. appreciating and experiencing a connectedness to all?

Knowing that we are not the ones in control all the time, that we pray to do G-d's will and have that will manifest in our daily lives is paradoxically a freeing experience. We admit that we are not the ones who are in control of every event, every day, or every person. We surrender our lives to the care of G-d, and ask only to be informed of that G-d's will and to have the strength to carry out what G-d asks and wants of us.

These are the Six Pathways to Personal Freedom.

Releasing the Physical, Mental, Emotional, Behavioral, Relational, and Spiritual blocks in our lives during Passover, we leave Egypt and our slave mentality and we are free.

Chapter 3

Letting Go of What No Longer Serves You

In this chapter you will learn and practice exercises that allow you to release what no longer serves you from each of the pathways presented.

Look again at the Whole Person model presented in the previous chapter, which identifies the Six Pathways to Personal Freedom. Working on these pathways via the exercises and worksheets following each chapter allows you to be who you are meant to be, authentic in your physical being, your thoughts, your feelings, your behaviors, your relationships, and your spirit.

We have begun to identify where in our lives we are still enslaved. Now we can turn to exercises to release our blocks to personal freedom.

Personal Freedom Tip

For all the work you do in this book, find a quiet, undisturbed location. Turn off your phone, and ask for n interruptions. I have found it helpful to choose the sam place each day, possibly the same time, as that way you body and mind go into your inner space easily, out of habits that you have now created.

Physical Clearing Exercises

Becoming Personally Free in our Physical Bodies and Spaces

Below are different physical clearing exercises. You can do them separately or all at once, whichever works for you. They are not meant to be done only once! Please return to any one of them that you particularly enjoy, and practice as the opportunity arises.

SITTING AND BREATHING

Begin by sitting quietly, allowing your eyes to close, and relaxing your muscles. Allow your attention to focus on your breathing. When you find your mind wandering, simply bring it back to the gentle rhythm of your breathing in and out. As you breathe in, think, "I breathe in well-being and cleansing." As you breathe out, think, "I release negativity and all blocks to my well-being."

Personal Freedom Tip

Some people find it helpful to use color as they breathe. What color signifies health and clearing to you? What color is negativity? For example: Picture a cleansing, healing white light entering your body, going to all your organs to purify and cleanse them. Watch as you breathe out and negativity leaves your body. Breathe in the cleansing white light again, and release the negativity with your breath out.

Breathe in and imagine your breath traveling through your body. Follow it as it goes from your lungs into your bloodstream, nourishing your organs and systems (your heart, your lungs, your stomach, your intestines, your liver, and your lymph nodes). Watch as your breath brings clearing and wellness to every part of your body. Release all negativity as you breathe out. See the spaces in your body that will receive only healing and good.

STANDING AND RELEASING

In a standing position: Stand with hands at your side. Relax and breathe gently in and out for a few moments. Inhale positive and healing energy. Now as you exhale, forcefully BLOW the air out through your mouth, picturing all negativity and that which you no longer need leaving your body. Breathe in and blow out in this manner several times, then again go back to gentle breathing in and out, picturing all that is good and healthy entering your body, all negativity leaving as you breathe out.

THROWING AWAY NEGATIVITY

Still standing, breathe in and raise your hands chest height, as if grasping objects in each fist. Now, think of what you wish to release, and, as you blow out, throw what you are "holding onto" far from you. Fling these with force, as far as you can. You may wish to think of something concrete that you are removing from your life and flinging far away, perhaps saying to yourself or out loud, "I release negative interactions from my life." "I let go of unhelpful thoughts and actions." "I am free of that which no longer serves me."

Shake it out! Stand, breathe, and feel the freedom and lightness in your body.

CLEARING HAMETZ FROM OUR ENVIRONMENT

Physical *hametz* includes that which we put into our bodies as well as what is in our environments. During *Pesach* we are told to rid our homes of all *hametz* as defined in Chapter I. We can expand that to include any food, drink, objects or substances that are not good for us. Perhaps you have identified consuming too much sugar in Worksheet #1. Your exercise can be to make a change in that area, choosing less sugar or sweeteners in your food. Changes in diet can be either gradual or extreme. Small changes can lead to other small changes and then build to bigger changes. Or, once you have cleared your shelves for *Pesach*, perhaps you will put back only foods that nurture you and lead to greater physical health. Cell phones and electronics can be major time-thieves and enslave us. Maybe it is time to take "phone and computer breaks" and experience the freedom that comes with that. A good place to start may be *Shabbat*, allowing yourself to be unplugged for 25 hours.

Return to a sitting position. Sit for a moment, following your breath in and out. Feel that you are lighter and freer physically.

Mental Clearing Exercises
Becoming Personally Free in our Thoughts

There are three exercises in this section. For these exercises, it is necessary to have a dedicated journal, document on your computer, or any means you wish to record your thoughts. That way you will have your thoughts all in one place and can return to see your progress.

REFUTING NEGATIVE THOUGHTS

Using Worksheet #2, (page 57) identify how you talk to yourself critically:

Perhaps you say, "I can't _____."

Write that in column 1 and look at it. Now allow your mind to refute that statement and write what you come up with in column 2.

For example:

Personal Freedom Tip

Notice your language and patterns as you do this exercise. Are there too many 'have to's? Is that action something you really WANT to do? Freedom lies in choice.

THOUGHT	REFUTATION
"I can't clear all the clutter from my house."	*I can start with one drawer, or room. I can do one task a day. What small area can I work on for 10 minutes?*
"I can't call X."	*Yes, I can, I just have to pick up the phone and do it. Do I want to? Is this someone I need to release from my life?*
"I'll never be able to do this."	*Why not? Do I need to ask for help? Do I really want to do it?*

Write several refuting statements for each negative statement you are saying to yourself.

JOURNALING

By writing down your thoughts using writing pages in this journal or any journal you wish to use, thereby allowing yourself to express them, you are getting them OUT of your body/ mind. Simply write whatever comes to your mind. Perhaps you will notice negative statements you need to refute, as in the above exercise. After you are done, you can save what you have written, re-read it, or burn it. You're a free person! It's up to you!

FINDING GRATITUDE

When you find yourself thinking about being irritated by someone's behavior, think of one thing, and then another, that you appreciate about that person. Allow yourself to be grateful they are in your life. Recognize there are reasons this person is in your life. Appreciate what you have learned (both positive and negative) by being in a relationship with that person. Perhaps what irritates you is a lesson that will help you grow or change. Recognize this person may not always be in your life, and appreciate that they are there now.

Sit for a moment, breathing in and out. Feel that your thoughts are clearer and you are lighter mentally.

Emotional Clearing Exercises
Becoming Personally Free with our Emotions

Before beginning the emotional clearing exercises, you must first recognize and feel your feelings. Once you've identified your emotions, take these steps:

JOURNALING

Carry a small notebook and jot down what you are feeling throughout the day. Note what you do with that feeling. Do you express that feeling, or do you just let it linger? How do you express it?

STATE YOUR FEELING(S) OUT LOUD

Say out loud, *"I am so happy right now!"* or *"I feel so angry!"*

Allow yourself to express your feelings and to hear yourself say them out loud, in your voice. Do this with a number of feelings throughout the day.

WRITE YOUR FEELINGS DOWN

Add your thoughts about them:

"X makes me so angry." Trace back your thoughts and feelings. Remember, thoughts create feelings; they do not just "pop up."

Personal Freedom Tip

Pay attention to your self-talk. What are you saying to yourself throughout the day? How you talk to yourself WILL influence how you feel.

Example: *I am so angry that X leaves their socks on the floor for me to pick up. I see the socks, I think to myself, "They don't value me," and I feel angry.*

In the above example: I see the socks on the floor and I think to myself, "G-d bless my spouse, they have their faults, but I'm glad we're together."

Personal Freedom Tip

You don't have to pick up the socks. Tell spouse they won't be washed unless they're in the hamper, and stick to that, or ask spouse to do their own laundry.

Sit for a moment, breathing in and out. Feel that you are lighter and happier in your thoughts. Smile to yourself and experience peacefulness.

Behavioral Clearing Exercises

Becoming Personally Free in our Behaviors

WRITE OUT THE BEHAVIOR YOU WISH TO CHANGE

Example: "I am pleasing others at my expense."

Note the triggers – the times, people, or events that encourage these behaviors. Especially take note of YOUR role – that is the only part you can change.

You cannot change the behavior of others, but *by changing your behavior, you invite them to change*, if they want to continue to relate to you. If you are doing the waltz and your partner starts to jitterbug, you need to change your steps, if you want to keep dancing with them, or they need to change theirs to continue to dance with you.[15]

IDENTIFY THE WAYS IN WHICH YOU CAN ALTER YOUR INTERACTIONS WITH OTHERS

For example:

A. I can ask people to change their behavior. Again your power is in your own behavior – not theirs. When x does ____, I will make them aware that it is upsetting to me, and ask if they are willing to do that differently. If not:

B. I can make a change in *my* behavior (how I choose to respond) and feel better.

C. I can change my thoughts about this. I can choose to interpret what this person is saying or doing in another way. I can try to see the situation from their vantage point.

---

15. Adapted from Harriet Lerner, *The Dance of Anger, A Woman's Guide to Changing the Patterns of Intimate Relationships* (New York: Harper Collins, 2014).

Sit for a moment, breathing in and out. Feel that you are lighter in your behaviors. Imagine some scenarios in which you will behave in a new way. Access your sense of humor. Perhaps you can smile when thinking about how you will now behave in any given situation.

Relational Clearing Exercises

Becoming Personally Free in our Relationships

It is important to be honest with yourself in looking at relationships. Look at what you have identified in the Relational section of Worksheet #1. How do I feel when I interact with X? Drained, depleted, frustrated, angry, bored? Or do I feel happy, amused, content, and at ease? Do I look forward to being with this person, attending this event, or do I feel burdened by them or it?

There are some relationships we have that we need to keep, even if they are not always enjoyable. But even with these, we have Personal Freedom choices. We can limit our time together or choose ways to spend time with that person in another way. For example, we may see them only with others around or, we can identify those situations where we enjoy their company and expand on those.

IDENTIFY HOW YOU FEEL WHEN YOU ARE WITH OTHERS

Examples:

"I feel frustrated and angry when X is critical of me or starts an argument."

"I feel overwhelmed by all that my boss asks me to do."

ACKNOWLEDGE THAT YOU HAVE CHOICES

A. Change your behavior: I will see X less often, I will breathe and relax when X is talking and not buy into an argument or criticism. I will see X only when I am with others who deflect behaviors that bother me. I will leave the room when that discussion starts. Or, I can speak to my boss and ask that they better define the parameters of my job.

B. Change your thoughts: Say to yourself, "I can listen without reacting," "That's their opinion, it really has nothing to do with me." Or simply notice the bothersome behavior and observe it saying, "Oh, there it is again," then breathe and let it go.

It is ok, and often necessary, to allow more distance from those who are not beneficial to your life.

Personal Freedom Tip

Personal freedom means it is within your power to choose with whom you will spend time, how much, how often, and the nature of your interactions. Who you have in your life is up to you!

Remember we are letting go of "*hametz.*" We are releasing that which no longer serves us from the pathways of our internal lives

Sit for a moment, breathing in and out. Picture a white light around you that protects you from boundary intrusions by others. Feel that you are freer in your relationships.

Spiritual Clearing Exercises
Finding Spiritual Freedom in Connection to the Universe

Until now we have focused on our bodies, minds, feelings, behaviors and interpersonal relationships. Now it is time to look at our connections to G-d and our universe. How do we acknowledge and experience that there is something beyond ourselves? How do we get in touch with the Divine?

The following are some suggestions:

SPEND TIME OUTSIDE AND IN NATURE

Use your breathing to breathe in energy from the trees, leaves, animals, grass, snow, or sunshine. Breathe in whatever in nature gives to you and energizes you. Feel these energies entering your body and soul.

GO OUTSIDE AT NIGHT AND GAZE AT THE STARS

Realize how vast the universe is, and allow its wonder to fill you. Feel the connection between you and all that surrounds you.

TAKE A WALK

Fill your lungs with good air. Think of negativity leaving you with each step and breath out. Picture all that is good around you filling your body and soul. Visualize yourself leaving the old ways behind you and walking into new ways of being in the world.

USE PRAYER

Express gratitude to G-d for all that is you and in your world. Ask G-d to remove obstacles from your life, in a way that is not too difficult for you.

If you are new to prayer and feel a bit uncomfortable, then express that to G-d. Start by speaking to G-d and saying, *"I don't know how to talk to you,"* *"This feels like more than I can handle, please help me,"* or *"I am willing to have G-d enter my life,"* and *"I accept G-d's will for my life."*

Personal Freedom Tip

Years ago I was more squeamish about flying. I wanted to let go of my fear of flying and prayed for G-d to remove that for me. We had a family ski vacation planned and, as happens in winter, there was a major storm. Flights were grounded by the time we got to Denver, and the only way we had to get to our destination was in a small 12 seater plane. We all got on board, and I spent the next hour or more flying in tears over the Rocky Mountains in prayer. DIFFICULT! But I certainly was helped past my fear of flying! Remember to ask that problems or obstacles be removed **in a way that is not too difficult for you.**

GIVE IT TO G-D

Some people like to use a "G-d Jar." Take a piece of paper, write on it what you wish to give to G-d, rather than handle alone. Put it in the jar or box, and it's done. It's in G-d's hands now.

Personal Freedom Tip

If you find yourself still ruminating about that, remind yourself that you have given that to G-d! It's no longer in your hands, let it go. Know that G-d is taking care of that.

PRACTICE FORGIVENESS

I like to think of the word "forgiveness" meaning that which is "FOR GIVING TO G-D." I can give that to G-d, and be free. I don't have to solve it or continue to think about it. And forgiving does not mean I continue to allow that behavior or person in my life. I can forgive and let go of X. Let go of whatever "it" is, and give "it" to G-d.

Sit for a moment, breathing in and out. Feel your connection to the universe and G-d. Allow the comfort of knowing all is in G-d's hands to calm your spirit.

These are the exercises you can put into place to experience personal freedom each year. This book is meant to be re-examined throughout the year, whenever you are reflecting on your inner world.

Chapter 4

"Ayeka?" Where Are You?

You now are familiar with the Six Paths to Personal Freedom. I hope you have followed some of the suggested exercises, so that you are feeling freer and lighter than before you read this book. It is now time to assess where you are.

Are you still in Egypt, not wanting to relinquish old ways and habits? Have you begun to think about the changes you wish to make? Are you letting go of former negative thoughts and behaviors and striving for a free person's mentality? Create for yourself a definition of Personal Freedom, or reread the definition of Personal Freedom at the beginning of this book and ask if you are approaching that.

It is my wish that this *Pesach* and every future *Chag Hamatzot* will bring you closer and closer to personal freedom. I hope you will use this book to continue to identify where you are throughout the year. Keeping a journal from *Pesach* to *Rosh Hashanah* will help you to assess your progress Maybe you will have even fewer *al cheyts* to say this year!

Remember that the Whole Person Wheel may be entered from any pathway, and that all pathways are interconnected. Moving and stretching can release tension in your body and send endorphins through your system helping you to feel more comfortable in your physical body. Simply sitting and paying attention to your breathing may bring you greater relaxation. Changing your thought processes from harsh and critical to kinder and more loving brings you increased feelings of contentment and improves your relationship with yourself and others. Looking at your behaviors objectively and asking if this still serves you will allow you to decide what to keep and what to release. Becoming more spiritually and positively connected to G-d, other people, and the universe will enhance your feelings of protection, community, and well-being.

I hope that you will share what you have learned with others either before or at your next Seder. You might want to introduce the concepts presented in this book, and ask people to think about where they are on the path to personal freedom. Draw or copy the Whole Person Wheel and ask people what being free in each of the sections means to them. How will they know they are leaving their personal *mitzrayim* and slaveries?

An interesting exercise for your journal is to ask yourself the following questions:

- What does freedom look like today? How will you know you are free?

- What will being physically free look like? How will I be moving? What will I be eating?

- What does mental freedom mean to me?

- How will I recognize that I am freer and more positive in my thinking?

- What will I do with my emotional life when I am free?

- How will I know I am feeling and expressing my emotions?

- What is behavioral freedom? What will that look like in my own behaviors?

- What is relational freedom? What relationships will I keep foremost in my life?

- Are there any relationships I need to distance from to feel happier and freer?

- How will I release or lessen these?

- And finally, what does spiritual freedom look like and feel like to me?

Please see Worksheets #3, #4, and #5 (pages 59-61), for further exploration of these questions and for extra journaling pages.

AYEKA? Where are you in your journey to freedom? It is my sincere hope that reading this book and doing the exercises will lead you to experience increased freedom now and in future years.

Conclusion

Dear Reader,

Thank you for allowing me to share my thoughts with you. This work has been a very long time coming. I have written and used these thoughts and worksheets as I worked with others in the secular field of personal growth over the past years.

Each year at *Pesach*, I have asked my own family and friends how they will experience leaving Egypt this year. What does being free mean?

Sometimes I was met with blank stares, sometimes there was a brief discussion before we proceeded with the Seder (Gotta eat, hungry!) It became clear to me that this type of thinking is not something to spring on people at the seder table.

Because we are always changing and evolving, perhaps returning to this book prior to *Pesach* each year will stimulate new thinking, new conversations, new experiences of freedom for you and your guests.

I hope that participating in the exercises suggested provides growth for you, and that you will let me know what you experience with this work.

I am happy to engage with you as well as provide workshops or discussions with your synagogue prayer or study groups. Please see "How to get in touch with the author" at the end of this book..

With all good wishes and blessings for your journey,

Katherine Englebardt

Gratitudes

I am forever grateful to all my teachers, particularly to those in my early Hebrew school years at The Park Synagogue in Cleveland Heights, Ohio. It was they who first awakened in me a deep love of the Jewish religion, with all its rituals, beliefs, and philosophies. Unlike many of my classmates who dreaded Hebrew school, I enjoyed attending classes and helping to lead our Junior Congregation. Ms. Loretta Roth was especially inspiring to me and nurtured the love we shared of Judaism. The stories and concepts we discussed, as well as the mystical teachings behind the Hebrew letters and notations, always fascinated me and compelled me to study and understand more.

The following rabbis were essential to my experiences, and I thank them: Rabbi Armond Cohen and Rabbi Sol Landau (both obm), from Park Synagogue, Cleveland Heights, Ohio, and Rabbi Samuel Kieffer, Rabbi Jon Konheim, Rabbi Robert Kasman, Rabbi Ted Lichtenfeld, and Rabbi Rafi Spitzer, from Congregation Agudat Achim, Schenectady, NY.

I am also grateful to those who came before me and now rest in peace: The Maggid of Kohzeniece (my great-grandfather x5), whose spirit I believe has led me to where I am today, the writings of Rabbi Jonathan Sacks, as well as Rebbe Nachman of Bratslav, Rav Kook, and Rebbe Menachem Schneerson, of blessed memory.

Much gratitude to my friends who have joined me in countless conversations and probings, and for the enjoyment of our lively spiritual debates and discussions.

Thank you to my readers, Mimi Becker, Ph.D., Janie Garnett, M.S., Barbara Liss Wolfe, BA, and Rabbi Rafi Spitzer, of Congregation Agudat Achim, Schenectady, New York. Your help has been immeasurably valuable in assuring that my words and exercises were understandable and *halachically* correct.

I am indebted to my editor, Karen Knowles, for her reading and re-reading of this manuscript and her excellent suggestions; to Nechama Dina Laber, publisher of Jewish Girls Unite Press, and Leah Caras, who created the design and made the book a physical reality.

Much gratitude to my coach, Susan Lowenthal Axelrod, whose knowledge, directness, positive energies and belief in me has allowed me to produce this book.

You have brought my words out of my head and heart and onto the page—our major goal! Through our weekly phone meetings and intermediary conversations, you fueled me when my energies were lagging and I always left our time together feeling uplifted and motivated.

Finally, my deepest love and thanks to my husband, Carl, for always nurturing my growth and allowing me the time and space to write uninterrupted. I am grateful for our wonderful children and grandchildren for being who they each are. You have helped shape me into who I am today and have encouraged my self-actualization and health always.

My love and gratitude to you all. I am blessed to have you in my life.

Appendix

THE WHOLE PERSON WHEEL

Adapted from work by Sharon Wegsheider-Cruse

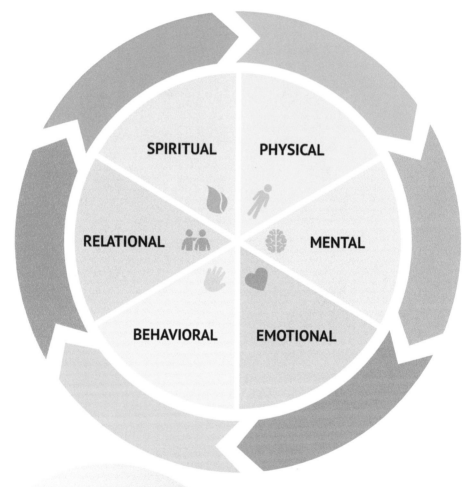

Personal Freedom Tip

Make a larger copy of this wheel with the different pie shapes. In each sector, write out examples from your life. Observe how all is interconnected and where you wish to begin to make changes.

WORKSHEET #1

Identifying Hametz in our physical, mental, emotional, behavioral, relational, and spiritual selves.

PHYSICAL: How do I experience my body? Do I feel heaviness, excess, pain, burdens, lack of movement, exercise? What about my environment? Is it cluttered? What can I release?

_____

_____

_____

_____

MENTAL: What is my thinking? Is it negative, critical, defeatist?

_____

_____

_____

_____

EMOTIONAL: What am I feeling? How do I express that?

_____

_____

_____

_____

BEHAVIORAL: How do my thoughts and feelings express themselves in my behaviors? Ex: *When I think A, I feel B, and I behave C. I isolate, gossip, lie, act cruelly, overdo, people please, ignore my own needs.*

RELATIONAL: Who is in my life? Are they toxic people vs. those who are kind and considerate?

SPIRITUAL: Do I feel a connection to G-d?; Are there blocks to my meditation, prayer or feeling connected to the universe, where, when, how?

WORKSHEET #2: EMOTIONAL CLEARING

Identifying the link between thoughts and feelings

EVENT	THOUGHT	FEELING
X says something	*"Nothing I do is good enough"*	*dismay, sadness*
See wounded dog on TV	*"That is horrible"*	*sadness, anger*
Learn I got a raise at work	*"WOW!"*	*happy, excited*

Identify some of your experiences:

EVENT	THOUGHT	FEELING

WORKSHEET #3

How will I know that I am making progress toward freedom?

PHYSICALLY: _____

_____

_____

MENTALLY: _____

_____

_____

EMOTIONALLY: _____

_____

_____

BEHAVIORALLY: _____

_____

_____

RELATIONALLY: _____

_____

_____

SPIRITUALLY: _____

_____

_____

WORKSHEET #4

What will I take out of Egypt? What will I leave behind?

I wish to keep: _____

_____

_____

_____

_____

_____

_____

_____

I will leave behind: _____

_____

_____

_____

_____

_____

_____

WORKSHEET #5

How Do I Define Personal Freedom?

I will know I am experiencing more personal freedom when I: *(write out your concrete, specific, observable behaviors that will tell you that you are becoming more free.)*

PHYSICALLY: _____

_____

_____

MENTALLY: _____

_____

_____

EMOTIONALLY: _____

_____

_____

BEHAVIORALLY: _____

_____

_____

RELATIONALLY: _____

_____

_____

_____

SPIRITUALLY: _____

_____

_____

_____

Notes & Reflections

62 "In Every Generation"

Guided Meditation

You may wish to record this to hear in your own voice, or sit in your uninterrupted quiet space and read.

PERSONAL FREEDOM

A Meditation to Soothe Your Soul (2020)
By Susan Lowenthal Axelod

Take this moment to breathe, deep breath in and long breath out. If you are comfortable, close your eyes so you can close out any external distractions. Now, breathe again, deep breath in and long breath out. And again, slow deep breath in and long breath out.

Find a quiet space inside you, it's there if you see it. It's a place of calm, of comfort, of safety. It may feel elusive, and that's ok. Gently keep seeking, keep searching, look actively even if you can only peek in. Breathe again now and enter that place. Now, it's all you in there. No pressures, no lights, no bells going off, no obligations, no worries or anxieties, not even any fears. All is at bay, with you on the beach just sitting quietly, comfortably and observing.

You, on the beach, looking at an ocean; water gently rising and falling as far as the eye can see. You watch as the water swirls and twirls, rises and falls and you see with amazement how it finally laps to the shore, a harmless, thin quiet layer of foamy iridescent spray gently coming to a full stop and then quietly receding, receding, receding.

If the idea of an ocean is a disconnect for you for any reason, see a great lake or even a country pond. Any visual of water that serves. Water, an infusion of senses about your life; water, life itself. Breathe again, now, gentle deep breath in and long breath out.

This is your quiet space, commit to finding it and go there. Choose the feeling of it, choose the way it looks in your mind's eye, choose the way it smells when you take in a breath and choose the way it sounds now that you have gotten quiet enough to listen.

This place is a place where you feel buoyant, weightless, free. You can imagine yourself in the water, surrounded by the lifeforce, bobbing or floating, weightless. *This* is freedom. This is your Personal Freedom. No restrictions or constrictions, no pain, no worries, no attachments to old ideas, no tethering to old habits. Just quiet, calm, safe; freedom. *This* is your Personal Freedom. Can you sense it? Can you feel it? Can you see, smell and hear it? This is your Personal Freedom.

This is where you are free to be you, the innermost you, the carefree, confident you. You, connected with your most authentic self, the place of your Soul. In your quiet contemplation, now, consider your Soul. Your Soul, your place of deepest feeling; the safest place of all to allow yourself to feel, to be; your place of Personal Freedom. Can you feel it? Can you sit there comfortably, allowing it to just be so? *This* is your place of Personal Freedom. There when you want it, there when you need it; always able to be accessed because it's always in you. In that quiet space you can seek out anytime. And, it finds you easily any time you are in, near or even around water. Any flowing water can be your reminder, even the blessing of water flowing from a faucet can be an experiential reminder of the Personal Freedom that lives in you. There with your Soul, there for the seeking, there, at any moment. Personal Freedom is yours, there when you're ready.

—Susan L. Axelrod, CCP, CFRE | 518.495.4573

REFERENCES

Axelrod, Susan Lowenthal. *Meditations to Ease, Calm and Inspire.* East Greenbush: JGU Press, 2019.

Axelrod, Susan Lowenthal. *Your Job is to Be: An Anthology to Inspire Soul Connection.* East Greenbush, JGU Press, 2018.

Cordoza, Arlene Rossen. *Jewish Family Celebrations.* New York: St. Martin's Press, 1982.

Goldberg, Rabbi Nathan. *Passover Haggadah, New Revised Edition.* Hoboken: Ktav Publishing House, 1993.

Greenberg, Irving. *The Jewish Way: Living the Holidays.* New York: Touchstone Books, 1988.

Greenberg, Sidney and Pamela Roth Eds. *In Every Generation ~ A Treasury of Inspiration for Passover and the Seder.* Northvale: Jason Aronson, Inc., 1988.

Lieber, David L., Sr. Editor. *Etz Chayim, Torah and Commentary.* New York: The Jewish Publication Society, 1985.

Lerner, Harriet. *The Dance of Anger, A Woman's Guide to Changing the Patterns of Intimate Relationships.* New York: Harper Collins, 2014.

Olitzky, Rabbi Kerry M. *Preparing Your Heart for Passover.* Philadelphia: The Jewish Publication Society, 2002.

Robinson, George. *Essential Judaism, A Complete Guide to Beliefs, Customs, and Rituals.* New York: Pocket Books, 2000.

Steinsalz, Adin. *The Essential Talmud.* London: Weidenfeld and Nicolson, 1976.

Wegsheider-Cruse. *Another Chance, Hope and Health for the Alcoholic Family.* Palo Alto: Science and Behavior Books, Inc., 1981.

ABOUT THE AUTHOR

Katherine Englebardt is a licensed Clinical Social Worker who is retired from a private psychotherapy practice treating adolescents and adults, individually and as couples and families. She has offered numerous workshops throughout the Capital District on Stress Management, Parenting, Fibromyalgia, and Recovery from Codependency.

Katherine's passion and focus have been on mind-body-spiritual connections with a major emphasis on communication. Specifically, she has applied material from her Masters Degree in Speech and Language Communications regarding the importance of language, especially how we speak to ourselves and others, and the effect that has on our mental, physical, and spiritual aspects of our beings.

As a Jewish woman and student, Katherine has studied and applied Jewish philosophy, rituals, prayer, meditation, music, and movement to enhance one's life.

A past president of Congregation Agudat Achim in Schenectady, New York, Katherine is proud of her work on the *"Elul Project,"* which she co-authored with Rabbi Jon Konheim and congregant Alice Rudnick. This joint effort was awarded a Gold prize in "Prayer and Ritual" category by the United Synagogue of Conservative Judaism in 1999. Please contact the author, if you are interested in obtaining a copy of this work.

Katherine lives in Niskayuna, NY, with her husband, Carl. They are the parents of three grown children and their spouses and significant others, Terra and Turner, Sam and Megan, and Ezra and Wendy. They are delighted to be grandparents to Josh, Oliver, and Jasper.

HOW TO GET IN TOUCH WITH THE AUTHOR:

I am excited to share this work with you and your community, and would love to hear how using these worksheets have supported your journey to personal freedom. If you wish to offer feedback (that would be great!) or to contact me via email, please write to: kenglebardt@gmail.com.